Spotlight on Kids Can Code

Understanding Coding with
JAVASCRIPT

Michael Sabatino

PowerKiDS press
New York

Published in 2018 by The Rosen Publishing Group, Inc.
29 East 21st Street, New York, NY 10010

Copyright © 2018 by The Rosen Publishing Group, Inc.

All rights reserved. No part of this book may be reproduced n any form without permission in writing from the publisher, except by a reviewer.

First Edition

Editor: Melissa Raé Shofner
Book Design: Michael J. Flynn

Photo Credits: Cover Jose Luis Pelaez Inc/Blend Images/Gety Images; p. 4 https://commons.wikimedia.org/wiki/File:Brendan_Eich_Mozilla_Foundation_official_photo.jpg; p. 5 Sergey Maksienko/Shutterstock.com; p. 7 FatCamera/E+/Getty Images; p. 9 racorn/Shutterstock.com; p. 11 (top) sabrisy/Shutterstock.com; p. 11 (bottom) 1000s_pixels/Shutterstock/com; p. 12 Dragon Images/Shutterstock.com; p. 13 Teguh Jati Prasetyo/Shutterstock.com; p. 21 vgajic/E+/Getty Images.

Library of Congress Cataloging-in-Publication Data

Names: Sabatino, Michael, author.
Title: Understanding coding with JavaScript / Michael Sabatino.
Description: New York : PowerKids Press, [2018] | Series: Spotlight on kids can code | Includes bibliographical references and index.
Identifiers: LCCN 2017003086| ISBN 9781508154785 (6 pack) | ISBN 9781508155256 (pbk.) | ISBN 9781508155133 (library bound)
Subjects: LCSH: JavaScript (Computer program language)–Juvenile literature. | HTML (Document markup language)–Juvenile literature. | Internet programming–Juvenile literature. | Web sites–Authoring programs–Juvenile literature.
Classification: LCC QA76.73.J39 S24 2018 | DDC 005.2/762–dc23
LC record available at https://lccn.loc.gov/2017003086

Manufactured in the United States of America

CPSIA Compliance Information: Batch #BS17PK: For Further Information contact Rosen Publishing, New York, New York at 1-800-237-9932

Contents

The Language of the Web............4
A Key Ingredient..................6
Follow the Rules..................8
Plays Well with HTML.............10
Terms to Know...................12
Let's Get Coding!................14
Making the Call..................18
Game Plan........................20
Just the Beginning...............22
Glossary.........................23
Index............................24
Websites.........................24

The Language of the Web

Have you ever played a game or looked at a slideshow of pictures online in your **web browser**? If so, then you've likely visited a web page that uses JavaScript. JavaScript is a popular programming language that brings web pages to life. From games to entire business **applications** such as word processors and spreadsheets, it's hard to imagine the World Wide Web without it.

In the mid-1990s, coder Brendan Eich wrote Mocha, which was an early **version** of JavaScript. In the early days of the Internet, web pages were mostly basic text files, which were static, or unchanging. Early web pioneers wanted a way to make web pages more dynamic and interactive. That required a new programming language made specifically with web pages in mind. The result was JavaScript. Today, JavaScript is used to create all sorts of online programs that run through web browsers.

Brendan Eich

JavaScript went through a few name changes. When Eich created it in May 1995, it was known as Mocha. It was later renamed LiveScript. In December 1995, it received its final name of JavaScript.

A Key Ingredient

In 1995, JavaScript first appeared in an early version of Netscape Navigator, one of the first web browsers. Since that time, JavaScript has become a necessary part of all popular web browsers today. Along with HTML and Cascading Style Sheets (CSS), JavaScript is one of the main parts of modern website design. Programmers use HTML, CSS, and JavaScript to create web pages that users can interact with by using a mouse and keyboard or a touchscreen. However, of those three main parts, only JavaScript is considered a true programming language.

By using lines of code made up of words and symbols, web designers can use JavaScript to create interactive pages for website visitors. A page may be able to detect mouse clicks, keystrokes, and much more. This allows web pages to respond to users with pop-up messages, moving images, sounds, and videos.

JavaScript can work on most computers, even if they're not connected to the Internet.

Follow the Rules

Before you can begin to learn about coding in any language—including JavaScript—you need to know that computer programming is about following rules. This makes writing computer code a lot like playing a game, and it can be just as much fun.

Rule 1: Coders must know what they want the computer to do and write a plan.

Rule 2: Coders must use special words to have the computer accept **input**, make choices, and take action.

Rule 3: Coders need to think about what tasks can be put into a group.

Rule 4: Coders need to employ **logic** using AND, OR, NOT, and other key words.

Rule 5: Coders must explore the **environment** and understand how it works.

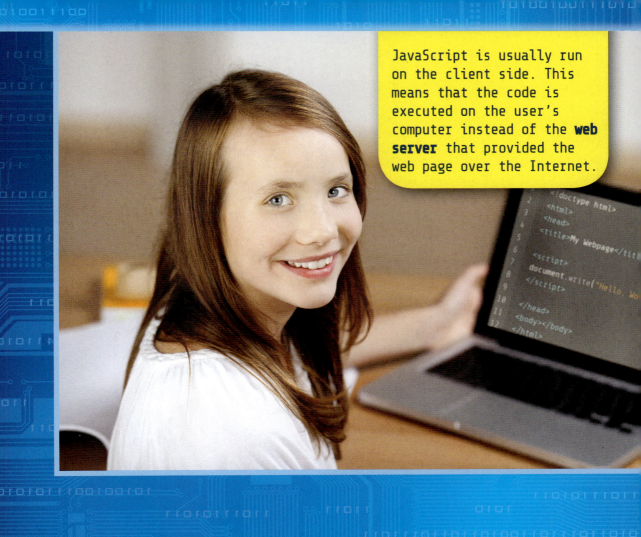

JavaScript is usually run on the client side. This means that the code is executed on the user's computer instead of the **web server** that provided the web page over the Internet.

Breaking the Code

Many programming languages, such as Scratch and Hopscotch, require a GUI (GOO-ee), or graphical user interface, in order to write code. "Graphical" refers to graphics, which are pictures and shapes. An "interface" is a way two things—such as a computer and a user—communicate with each other. However, JavaScript doesn't need its own GUI. It's a written-text language and can be created in any basic text-editor program.

Plays Well with HTML

JavaScript was designed to work closely with HTML. HTML is the standard language needed to create a web page. Web browsers convert HTML into what we see as web pages on computer screens. JavaScript is able to manipulate, or shape, all the HTML elements on a web page. This makes it a powerful tool for creating web applications.

Programmers can place JavaScript code right inside HTML code. When a web browser loads HTML to display a web page, it also executes, or runs, all of the JavaScript code it finds inside the HTML. Web browsers execute the JavaScript code in the order in which it appears. This means JavaScript code in the beginning of the HTML is executed before code near the end. A common use for JavaScript is to let users know if they made an error while filling out a form online.

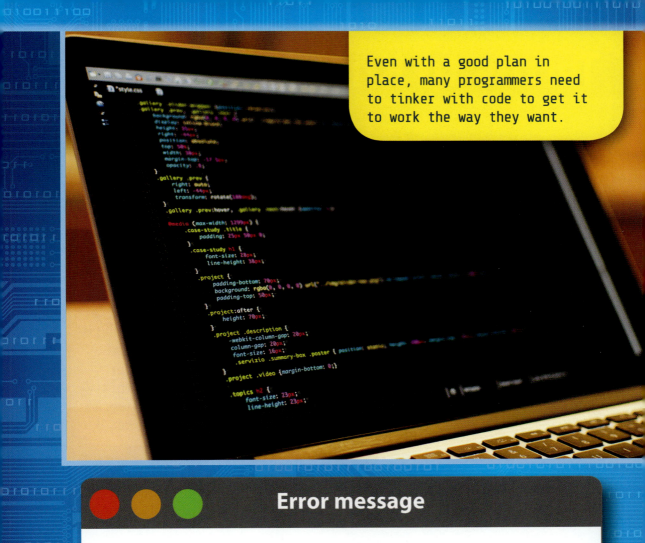

Even with a good plan in place, many programmers need to tinker with code to get it to work the way they want.

Error message

Error!

Cancel

Terms to Know

Coding isn't just for computer specialists. Anyone can do it! Before we run through a few examples, here's a helpful list of terms you'll need to understand. You'll be coding with JavaScript in no time!

You don't have to be an expert—or even an adult—to learn how to code. Check to see if your school or local library offers a coding program and get started today!

alert: A built-in JavaScript function that shows a message to the user in a pop-up window.

code library: Prewritten code that performs commonly used tasks to save time when creating a program.

function: Reusable code that performs a task and can be used repeatedly in a program.

HTML event: Something the user or browser does that causes code to execute.

HTML tag: A single building block of a web page.

pop-up window: A smaller window inside the larger web browser window that is often used to display messages to the user.

write: A built-in JavaScript function that writes text on the screen in the web browser.

Let's Get Coding!

It's easy to start coding with JavaScript. All you need is a simple text editor and a web browser. Most computers already have these programs installed, or set up for use. The text editor is where you write and save your code as a file with a .html **extension**. The .html extension tells the browser that it should display the file as a web page. Any JavaScript code in the .html file will run when that file is opened in the web browser.

The first program that many new coders learn is the Hello World program. This is because it's an easy way for beginners to get their feet wet with a new programming language. Here's an example of an HTML file with JavaScript that displays "Hello, World!" on the screen when it's opened in a web browser.

The HTML tags `<script>` and `</script>` instruct the web browser to treat the text that appears between them as JavaScript code. In this example, `document.write("Hello, World!");` is the JavaScript code that gets executed.

```html
1   <!doctype html>
2   <html>
3   <head>
4   <title>My Webpage</title>
5
6   <script>
7   document.write("Hello, World!");
8   </script>
9
10  </head>
11  <body></body>
12  </html>
```

Breaking the Code

You can execute your JavaScript code by simply opening the HTML file containing your code in a browser. Once the file is loaded, you can hit the browser's refresh button to execute the code again.

The previous example used a JavaScript function called "write." Functions are common to many programming languages and are important building blocks in most applications. They do specific things and are usually named after the tasks they perform. For example, the "write" function instructs the web browser to write words on the web page.

In the next example, we'll use another JavaScript function to show "Hello, World!" in a different way. This time, instead of using the "write" function, we'll use the "alert" function. When this code is run, the JavaScript function "alert" tells the browser to alert the user with a pop-up window that displays a message. Here, the message is our same "Hello, World!" text. An alert usually requires the user to click an "OK" button in the pop-up window before they can do anything else on the web page.

Spelling and capitalization matter when writing code. If you aren't **consistent**, your code won't work properly.

```
1   <!doctype html>
2   <html>
3   <head>
4   <title>My Webpage</title>
5
6   <script>
7   alert("Hello, World!");
8   </script>
9
10  </head>
11  <body></body>
12  </html>
```

Breaking the Code

Functions can accept parameters. A parameter is a bit of information that the code inside the function can use to perform its task. In this example, we're passing the text "Hello, World!" to the alert function as a parameter. The alert function's task is to display its parameter in a pop-up window.

Making the Call

You can write your own functions in JavaScript. In the next example, we'll code our own function called "sayCheese." We'll use it to create a program that displays "Cheese!" when a user clicks a button on our web page.

Here, we're using the HTML <button> tag to create the button. Within this tag, there's a special command called "onClick." This instructs the browser to "call" our custom-made function "sayCheese" whenever a user clicks that button. The phrase "call a function" means to make the code inside of that function execute. To put it all together, clicking the button will trigger the call to our "sayCheese" function, which then executes the familiar alert function inside of it. Similar to the last example, the alert will then display "Cheese!" to the user in a pop-up window.

The command "onClick" is one of several HTML events. An event is something the user or web browser does that prompts JavaScript code to execute.

```html
1    <!doctype html>
2    <html>
3    <head>
4        <title>My Webpage</title>
5
6    <script>
7    function sayCheese ()
8    {
9        alert("Cheese!");
10   }
11   </script>
12
13   </head>
14   <body>
15   <button onClick="sayCheese();">Say cheese!</button>
16   </body>
17   </html>
```

Breaking the Code

It's good practice to use **descriptive** names for the functions you create yourself. This makes your code easier to understand.

19

Game Plan

When you're ready to create your own JavaScript program, here are the steps to follow:

```
1. Write out a simple plan for your program.
2. Open your text editor and create a file with
     a .html extension.
3. Type the following HTML code in the file:
<!doctype html>
<html>
<head>
<title>My Web page</title>
<script>
</script>
</head>
<body>
</body>
</html>
4. Type your JavaScript code between the <script>
     and </script> HTML tags.
5. Save the file.
6. Open the file in a web browser to run your code!
```

If you make any changes to the code, be sure to save the file again before you run it in the browser. Any changes you make won't show in the browser unless you save the file first. Once you have your HTML file open in a web browser, you can hit the refresh button each time you'd like to rerun the code. This is handy if you're making lots of changes to your code.

There are lots of online resources to help you learn more about coding. Some websites even provide step-by-step instructions and let you practice coding right on their page.

Just the Beginning

JavaScript is a good language for programmers who are just starting out. Many helpful websites offer guides and examples that you can try on your own. In addition, JavaScript's **syntax** is similar to other more **complex** and powerful programming languages, such as C++ and Java. If you're familiar with JavaScript, you may find it's easier to learn other programming languages.

Today, there are many JavaScript code libraries you can download to make building programs even faster and easier. You can download many JavaScript frameworks from the Internet for free. Frameworks are prewritten code that give you an orderly way of creating programs. These examples are just the beginning of what you can do with JavaScript. With a plan, a text editor, and a web browser, it's easy to start coding with JavaScript!

Glossary

application: A program that performs one of the major tasks for which a computer is used.

complex: Not easy to understand or explain.

consistent: Sticking with one way of acting or proceeding.

descriptive: Using words to give a picture.

environment: The combination of computer hardware and software that allows a user to perform various tasks.

extension: The last part of a filename that tells what kind of file it is, such as .txt or .docx.

input: Information that is entered into a computer.

logic: A proper or reasonable way of thinking about or understanding something.

syntax: How words are arranged to form a sentence.

version: A form of something that is different from the ones that came before it.

web browser: A computer program that allows users to search the Internet.

web server: A computer or computer program that dispenses web pages as they are requested.

Index

A
alert (JavaScript function), 13, 16, 17, 18

B
browser, web, 4, 6, 10, 13, 14, 15, 16, 18, 19, 20, 22

C
C++, 22
Cascading Style Sheets (CSS), 6
code library, 13, 22

E
Eich, Brendan, 4, 5
extension, 14, 20

F
frameworks, 22
function, 13, 16, 17, 18, 19

G
graphical user interface (GUI), 9

H
Hopscotch, 9
HTML, 6, 10, 13, 14, 15, 18, 19, 20
HTML event, 13, 19
HTML tag, 13, 15, 18, 20

J
Java, 22

L
LiveScript, 5
logic, 8

M
Mocha, 4, 5

N
Netscape Navigator, 6

P
parameter, 17
pop-up window, 13, 16, 17, 18

S
Scratch, 9
server, web, 9
syntax, 22

T
text editor, 9, 14, 20, 22

W
write (JavaScript function), 13, 15, 16

Websites

Due to the changing nature of Internet links, PowerKids Press has developed an online list of websites related to the subject of this book. This site is updated regularly. Please use this link to access the list: www.powerkidslinks.com/skcc/ucjs